Who Goes Splash?

AN EARLY BIRD BOOK™
By Sue Tarsky
Illustrated by Katy Sleight

Random House 🏠 New York

Who is climbing?
Who is digging?

Who is watering the garden?
Who is bathing in a puddle?

Who makes muddy footprints?

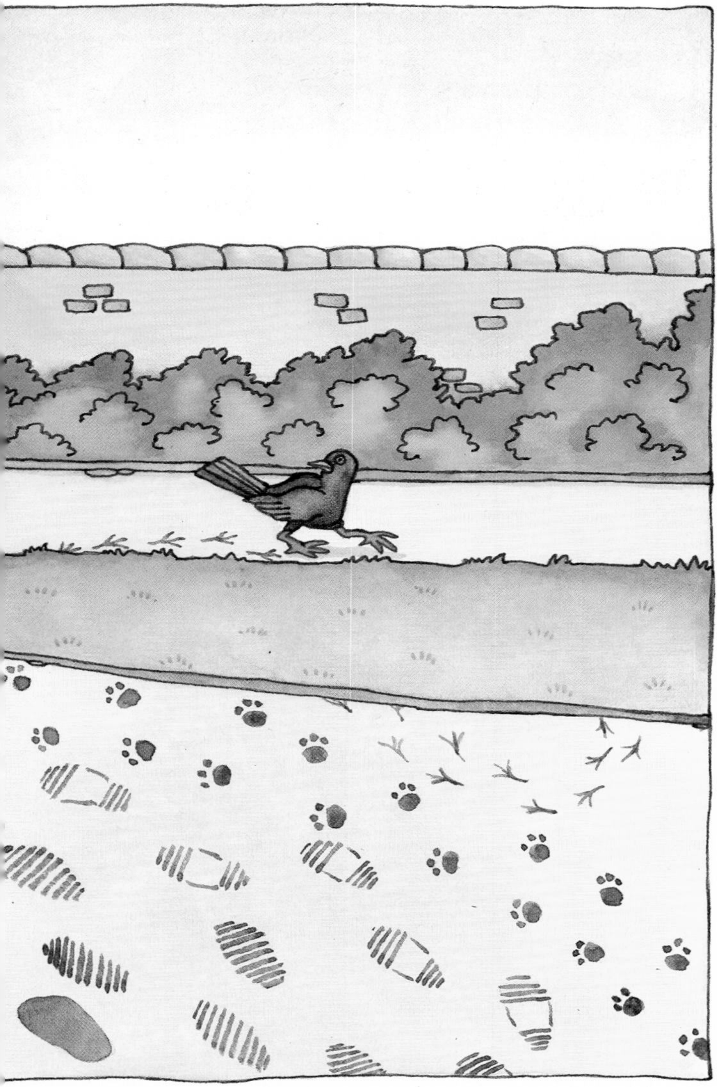

Who hops?
Who glides along the path?

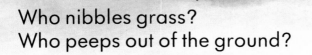

Who nibbles grass?
Who peeps out of the ground?

Who is hiding in the bushes?

What grows in a flower bed?

What do you grow
in a vegetable patch?

boot

tomatoes

lettuce

beans

What are the birds eating?
What is the dog eating?

What do you eat in the garden?

What is funny in this garden?

Who is swinging?
Who is sleeping?

Who is running?
Who is sitting on the clothesline?

What goes on
the clothesline?

What belongs in the sandbox?

Who likes splashing
in the pool?

Who barks? Who meows?
Who squeaks?
Who goes splash?